Priceless Pearls

Priceless Pearls

LaVerne Hayes Harris

Published by Omega Publishing Co.

Copyright © 2013 by LaVerne Hayes Harris

ISBN 978-0-615-77412-1
Manufactured in the United States of America

Published March, 2013

Book Production:
Marvin D. Cloud, mybestseller Publishing Company.
marvindcloud@marvindcloud.com

This book is dedicated to my husband Robert, son Shannon and daughter Rochelle who have faithfully supported every endeavor, every new adventure, and every project I chose to undertake. Thanks guys for allowing me the freedom to be me.

Acknowledgments

A special thanks to God for entrusting me with this project and for blessing me with the skills and talents necessary to complete it. I am honored that you chose me. I enjoyed writing with you.

Thank you to my spiritual leader and pastor, Bishop I.V. Hilliard of New Light Christian Center Church in Houston, Texas for teaching the uncompromising word of Faith and the spiritual principles shared herein.

I also want to express my sincere thanks to my dear friends Amelia Young, Joyce Thomas, Loretta Norris, and Marvin Cloud for all editing and production assistance you provided and for believing in my vision enough to lend a hand. I could not have done it without you.

I also give a hearty thanks to you, the reader, for purchasing this book. May it bless your life now and for years to come.

CONTENTS

Introduction

The idea for this book was initially born of a desire to leave a bit of myself for my children to enjoy years after my physical body was gone from their sight. I knew that life would present situations that would leave them searching for wisdom. Rather than leave them the task of seeking insight from unfamiliar sources, I chose instead to leave them a bit of my own personal wisdom in this special book, *Priceless Pearls*.

There is a proverb which says "a good man leaves an inheritance for his children and his children's children." As I pondered this idea I concluded that the greatest gift I could give my children was the gift of wisdom which I had gained over the years. When the writing was complete and final product shared with friends and family, all agreed that it was a book that would be beneficial to all readers.

While I readily admit that I do not have all the answers,   through the leading of the Spirit I can say that my steps have been ordered and my path has been blessed. For that reason, I willingly share that wisdom with all who are seeking guidance.

The topics chosen were near and dear to my heart because they were areas which I had to gain victory over at some point in my life. Many of the stories shared chronicle actual incidents where I had to apply the spiritual principles taught to me by my spiritual leader, Bishop. I.V. Hilliard. The bible teaches that knowledge is essential if we are to live an abundant life--otherwise, we will perish in our ignorance.

My objective in writing this book was to provide you, the reader, with
- Wisdom for Winning
- Wisdom for Inner Peace
- Wisdom for Spiritual Strength
- Wisdom for Relationships
- Wisdom for Increase

I am sure you will agree that the world around us is oftentimes confusing but I am convinced that God desires the best in life for us and wants us to prosper in every way--mind, body and spirit. Within these pages I trust that you will find wisdom that will empower you to tackle many of life's challenges and gain strength to help you move forward toward your destiny.

Wisdom for Winning

You were born with potential. You were born with goodness and trust. You were born with ideas and dreams. You were born with wings. Learn to use them and fly.

CHAPTER ONE

KNOW WHO YOU ARE

The old folks used to tell us, "Don't think too highly of yourself, or people won't like you"... they lied. I grew up in a small coastal town in south Texas in the 60's. I attended the local high school, made good grades, had lots of friends and did the usual things that teenagers do. I went to church regularly, thanks to my Mom. Upon casual observance, I was every bit the average kid. Yes, you would think so but not according to my Spirit. For as long as I could remember, I have had an inner voice that would constantly remind me I was special...that I was born to do great things. As a child I did not recognize it as the voice of my spirit but rather referred to it as "something said to me" or "my first mind told me."

I had an Aunt Grace who was also one of my high school teachers. She would often ask me "Girl, do you know who you are?" At the time I would respond with the obvious answer of "Yes, I am LaVerne, daughter of Howard and Catherine..." She would only shake her head at my shallowness and walk away. At the time I did not understand

5

what she was really asking me and she did not try to clarify the question for me. As the years passed, she eventually stopped asking me but the question continued to linger in my mind.

Knowing who God made you to be is the beginning of wisdom.

As I began to grow and mature spiritually, I eventually understood what she was asking me. She wanted to know if I knew my inner self; if I knew who I had been created to be. I now know that at the time, I did not have a clue. I thought I was just an average kid. Little did I know that I had been cut from a totally different cloth. As the years passed I became more knowledgeable of who I was and what I was created to be. I began to realize that in order for me to fulfill my potential as a child of God, I had to fully discover the gifts and purposes for which I had been created. There is a scripture which says that we are God's "workmanship." That simply means that we are a work in process, an unfinished product. As such, we must conclude that throughout our lives, God is eloquently shaping and molding us into what he wants us to be.

I can now say with confidence that I am today the woman that God intended me to be. Through Him, I know that I have been endowed with strength of character that transcends the norm. I have been given a level of compassion that allows me to reach out to people sincerely without pretense. Unconditional love ia placed within me that allows me to extend that love to others without compromise. I have a place of peace within me that shelters me from the storms of life. The labor of my hands is blessed and I am able to succeed at all that I do. I always rise to the head of the class, no matter where I am or where I go. My thoughts are sought after and my wisdom is respected. I am able to do great things.

Over my life, I have enjoyed many accomplishments which I count as notable. My greatness, however, has been in the fruit that I have borne—my children. So many people cannot look behind themselves and beam with joy at the children and grandchildren God has blessed them with. Fortunately, I am one of those who can. My children have been my greatest accomplishment. I can see in each of them a little bit of myself; a bit of the better part of me, placed carefully within them, providing a solid foundation for their own personal growth. The thing that I am most proud of is that when I ask the question," Do you know who you are?", they know the answer. I have sought over the years to instill within each of them the knowledge that they are by no means the "average" child; that they were born for greatness; that their destiny is limitless; and that their uniqueness will make them valuable to the world. The awesome thing is "They Believe Me"!! Praise God!

So, as you move toward you destiny, take time to become acquainted with and learn about the person you are now and the person you are destined to become. Perhaps you will say that you are unsure or unaware of who you are to be, but take confidence in the knowledge that he who began a good work in you is able to finish it. God is not finished with you yet so be encouraged.

THE PRAYER OF JABEZ

Oh, that you would bless me indeed and enlarge my territory. That Your hand would be with me, and that You keep me from evil, that I may not cause pain.

I Chronicles 4: 9-10 KJV

CHAPTER TWO

DON'T BE AFRAID ...
ASK FOR WHAT YOU
WANT

No matter where I go, I am constantly amazed at the number of people staring at and constantly fiddling with their cell phones, IPad's, tablets, smartphones, laptops or whatever new electronic gadget they have in their possession. For the most part they are reading, blogging, tweeting, emailing and texting about the intimate details of some other person's life. The TV shows provide the same type of entertainment. The networks are now overrun with a new phenomena called "Reality Shows" chronicling the lives of various individuals engaging in questionable activities. Nevertheless, they are watched vicariously by us because we think they possess something we would like to have—fame, fortune, love, power, success, etc. Well, those things are not just for some but are available to you as well.

Most of us have a desire to reach for a life containing more than what we currently have. It is not that we are totally ungrateful for the life we have been given. On the contrary, we have been taught as a culture to be grateful for whatever life has brought us and not to expect more. After all, if God wanted us to have more, wouldn't he have already given it to us? Unfortunately, the answer to that question is "Not Always!" God's will for our lives does not automatically come to pass. We must do something to start the flow of blessings into our lives.

> *Ask and it shall be given, seek and you will find, knock and the door will be opened.*
> *Luke 11:9 KJV*

The truth of the matter is that God really does have unclaimed blessings waiting for you. It is not self-serving or selfish to believe this. Your desire to have abundance in your life should be what springs you into action and enables you to proceed with the expectation that your blessings will come.

Be willing to ask for what you want, expecting an answer. To ask for a blessing is to ask for supernatural favor. That's favor beyond the norm...exceeding natural expectations. God's nature is to bless but there are some blessings that only come if you ASK. Even though there is no limit to God's goodness, if you did not ask for a blessing yesterday, you did not get all that you were entitled to. I have found that many times we will not go after the life we want because we really do not believe that we deserve it. Society and upbringing are two factors that feed into our image of how we expect our lives to be. My children grew up hearing me tell them that they could do anything, have anything and accomplish anything they desired. The only limitations they faced were those that were self-imposed. It was a matter of choice.

When you begin to ask for what you want, often-times doubt will enter in to try and deplete your faith. This is where trust, in a power that is greater than yourself, enters in. You do not doubt, from one minute to the next, that your heart will beat and blood will flow through your veins or that there will be sufficient oxygen to breathe. You simply trust that it will be so and go about your life accordingly. That same trust should extend to your belief in the provision of your "asked for" blessings. You simply trust that it is so and live your life in daily expectation.

Understand that unbelief will produce nothing. It is a bottomless cup from which nothing flows. It takes rather than gives. The only way to destroy its hold on your spirit is to ask, believing you will receive and begin to speak your desires into existence.

Let me put it another way. Why stand begging with a cup in your hand hoping to get just enough to make it through the day. Instead, *make your petitions known before the Lord and believe you will receive all that you need.* The currents of grace and wisdom will then be able to sweep you forward to that new wealthy place waiting for you.

We shape our lives, we mold ourselves. In the end, we have the potential for good or evil. The path we choose is ultimately our responsibility.

Chapter Three

Think Before You Choose

There is a phrase that I heard Bishop Hilliard use years ago and have often quoted to my children. It says "Life is choice driven. We live or die by the choices we make." The great thing about humanity is that we have been given the right to choose our path. Over time, we find that the right choice has its benefits. William Jennings Bryan wrote that "Destiny is not a matter of chance but a matter of choice..." Life simply does not just happen; it is created by the choices we make.

While I believe in divine appointment, I also know that we can alter our destiny with bad choices. Although it may be more convenient or comfortable to blame others for what occurs in our lives, the fact is that we control our destiny with the words of our mouth and the multitude of choices that we make each and every day.

Every waking moment, we are making choices. Today, we will choose what foods to put in our body. We will choose whether we exercise or sit in front of the TV. We will choose what we put in our minds.

We will choose the people with whom we will interact. We will choose whether we will treat others with kindness and compassion or hatred and disdain. We will choose whether to be happy or sad. We will, no doubt, make hundreds of other decisions that directly impact the quality of our life.

Some of the choices we make will have immediate impact. Others will have an impact days, or even weeks, later. But, make no mistake about it, the multitude of choices we make today will set the standards for our lives today and tomorrow.

I have often heard the phrase, *"If it is going to be, it is up to me."* Rather than suggesting some self-centered, ego based notion of life, this phrase sends forth the message of choice. There is another truth to be shared about making good choices. The undeniable fact is that making bad choices brings with it consequences that must be dealt with. Whether we choose to believe it or not, the "sowing and reaping" principle is still alive and well. We must, therefore, consider carefully the consequences of our actions and how our lives will be impacted. The choice is still up to us.

In order to live a victorious life we must first win on the battlefield of our minds. It matters not how rich or well known we are, our lives will be a reflection of the thoughts that plague our minds. We must make a choice to keep our minds focused on the higher things. We must make a quality decision to focus only on the good things that God has promised us. This is especially important during times of adversity because the tendency to doubt worry or be in fear is more prevelant, at that time, than ever before. We must, on purpose, choose to trust in God's promises and not allow ourselves to doubt or become discouraged.

When I heard for the first time the scripture instructing us to *"renew our minds daily and put on a fresh mental attitude."* I initially questioned why such action was necessary. It seemed logical that the same mindset should be useful from one day to the next. I have since learned that the mind is constantly at odds with the Spirit. It seeks to draw into itself those things which it conceives, whether good or bad. The Spirit speaks of good things and endless possibilities. The mind raises questions and seeks to limit our options. The Spirit gives life to our hopes and dreams. The mind will seek to rationalize and tell us why it cannot be done. It is therefore necessary that we *"cast down imaginations (of the mind) and bring every thought under our control."* *(II Corinthians 10:5 Amplified)* We must first recognize whose voice we hear. The voice of the mind , while capable of good thoughts, can sometimes be misleading. Listen, instead, for the voice of the Spirit who seeks to teach you all things needed to make good choices in life.

The universe responds to our greatest desires, thoughts and emotions. It is the stuff that fuels our dreams and fulfills our destiny.

CHAPTER FOUR

TAKE TIME TO DREAM

I recently heard a noted speaker tell the story of a little frog who lived in a well. He swam freely in the water at the bottom of the well and thought how lucky he was to have this vast supply of water for his own personal use. It was clean and clear and just about everything a frog could hope for. One day after surfacing to the top he looked up and saw a bright light at the top of the well. Being the curious frog that he was, he decided to hop to the top to see what it was. Inch by inch he made his way to the top of the well and gingerly peeked over. There were trees swaying in the breeze and brightly colored flowers all around. Not too far from the well was a pond. It was more water than he had ever seen in his life so he hopped out of the well to get a better look. He swam in the pond for a little while and thought to himself that he must be the luckiest frog in the world to have so much water to swim in. He happily swam from one side of the pond to the other.

He would have been perfectly content to stay in the pond except that being the curious frog that he was, he hopped away from the pond one day and came upon a lake. Again, he thought that this was the most water he had ever seen. There was water stretching for a long way to another shore barely visible on the other side. He made lots of friends in the lake but being the curious frog that he was, he hopped away from

Don't be afraid of the space between dreams and reality. If you can dream it and believe it, you can achieve it.

the lake one day and soon came upon an ocean.

There was so much water that he could not see to the other side. Water seemed to go on for miles as far as the eyes could see. As he thought back to the water in the well, he realized that had he not been brave enough to hop away from his safe little well, he never would have known that there was an ocean of endless possibilities waiting for him.

The moral of this story is to take some time each day and allow your mind to survey the endless possibilities that await you. Use this time to consider those things which seem to be impossible to achieve. Expand your thinking to include those dreams and desires hidden deep within your heart. A great writer said *"As a man thinketh, so is he." (Proverbs 23:7 KJV)* Know that you are only limited by the barriers you create in your own mind. Like the frog you must be willing to step away from what is comfortable and press toward something greater. Know that it is your time.

God wants to plant new ideas in your heart and paint them on the canvass of your imagination. He wants you to cast off those old barriers to success and burst forth with new ideas, inspiration and knowledge of witty inventions. There is a spiritual principle which says we move toward what we can see in our minds. If all we can see are the restrictive circumstances surrounding us, then we will continue to move within those restrictive circles. If, on the other hand, we allow ourselves to look beyond where we are to where we want to be, our faith can then move us toward achieving what we believe.

I encourage you to dare to dream and start seeing yourself as the recipient of God's blessings. Expect the favor of God. Expect promotions and increase. Expect health and wealth. If you live in faith, always abounding in the things of God, you can trust Him to take you places you have never been and to fulfill all of your dreams.

Happiness is like a butterfly, the more you chase after it, the more it will elude you; but if you turn your attention to other things, it will come and sit quietly on your shoulder.

CHAPTER FIVE

FOLLOW YOUR BLISS

I am quick to grab on to witty slogans and mind stimulating euphemisms. I was listening to a TV talk show recently and the host began to encourage the listeners to "follow their bliss." I immediately realized that he was talking about pursuing those things that made them happy which is a concept I fully support. I have always told my children when they were trying to make a career decision, "do what makes you happy and you will never view it as work again."

It is never too late to "follow your bliss." Perhaps you did start out allowing the noise of other people's suggestions to silence your own inner voice. The question to consider now is "What inspires you?" What is it that you would love to do more than anything else? Consider your answer carefully because real success comes when you are acting on that inspiration.

Be mindful that as you decide upon that thing that inspires you and start to put into action that great idea, there will be a little voice in your mind which will say "You can't do that"or "you don't have what it takes to accomplish that." It will be said with such conviction that you will almost be tempted to believe it. It will remind you of the limitations, obstacles and roadblocks in your way. Don't believe it! Get a vision of what is possible for you and go

> *Stand in the door to your destiny and boldly take every step—large and small—with courage and intent.*

after it with the determination necessary to suceed.

God has given you gifts, talents, and interests. When you follow your dreams and listen to the voice within, the abundance of the universe unfolds. You must come to a place of trust and faith to believe that "When you delight yourself in Him, He will give you the desires of your heart." This does not necessarily mean that he will give you everything that you desire because all desires are not good. Instead, it means that God will place His desires for your life within your heart and give you the ability to accomplish them. You will then be able to concentrate on doing those things that make you happy and give you peace. **So go ahead, follow your bliss, do what you love and get out of your own way.**

Wisdom for Inner Peace

You don't need a formal prayer or tearful plea to bring the angels to your side. Simply say, "Angels, surround me", and they are there.

CHAPTER SIX

CALL ON YOUR ANGELS DAILY

L ike every other child, I grew up with nursery rhymes and fairy tales that spoke of mystical beings with the ability to move between the physical and spiritual realms effortlessly. Among these were Santa Clause, The Tooth Fairy, the Easter Bunny, and of course, Angels. On Sundays I would listen as the preacher told biblical stories of angels that appeared to Mary, that wrestled with Jacob, that ministered to Jesus, that spoke to Abraham, Sarah, Martha, and many more. At that time, they were just that...stories. As I matured and began to read my bible and develop a relationship with God through prayer, He slowly began to reveal Himself to me. He is so infinite and transcendent. Knowledge of His will, His word, and His wisdom encompasses so much of me that every second with Him is a learning experience. So it was and has been with the revelations that came to me concerning angels.

The word in I Corinthians 2: 9-10 (Living Bible) says *"That is what is meant in the Scriptures when it says that no man has ever seen, heard or even imagined*

*what wonderful things God has ready for those who love
the Lord. But we know about these things because God
has sent his Spirit to tell us and his Spirit searches out and
shows us all of God's deepest secrets."* Knowledge of the
existence of angels is one of those secrets God reveals
to those who love Him.

With God, some knowledge is only on a "need to
know" basis. When you consider the breadth and
depth of knowledge the Bible imparts, you almost
stagger under the weight of it. God says "for such a
time as this" as a way of explaining how and when
certain knowledge is revealed by his Spirit to us......
what we need comes when we need it.

In a chaotic world, it is no wonder that God has
made provision to send guides and messengers to
bring us help in troubled times. It is his nature to care
for his children as any loving father would. Although
he is omnipresent, his angelic messengers are available
to provide immediate assistance whenever they are
instructed to. People of faith have called them guard-
ians which I believe is an apt description as they do
guard and protect. In order to fully understand who
these messengers are, we must first examine their
nature and purpose.

It is not unusual for a person who has lost a loved
one to say " I know my mom is near even though she
died last year. I can feel her presence watching over
me. She has become my guardian angel." While
this is a sweet notion, it is in fact not the working of
actual angels. Angels are not the recreated spirits of
people who have deceased. They are not people at
all. The scripture speaks of how God created angels
before he created either heaven or earth or mankind.

Angels were a separate creation and their purpose was threefold—to worship God, to deliver his word, and then guard us.

If you noticed, I said "us." I did not say only the "believers." The scriptures say that God loves the saint and the sinner, the good and the bad. In that manner, I believe that we all have angels assigned to us who "guard us in all our ways." (Psalms 91 KJV) Does it always save us from disaster or destruction? No... because many will not hear God's voice or hearken to the spiritual warnings that are given. Part of God's loving us is to allow us to reap the consequences of our behavior. The Word says that "with each temptation, he will make a way of escape..." Unfortunately, many do not take the escape route and therefore do not get out of the trouble they are in.

I can remember as a child hearing of instances where people believed that they had encountered an angel who spoke to them or helped them in some way. Like a child, it was only one of those things that made you say "Hmmm!" because in your skeptical mind, it may or may not have happened. God, however, has a way of taking seemingly insignificant things to totally change the fabric of our belief system.

In my 20's I came across a copy of the book "The Divine Romance" in my church bookstore. This book was the author, Gene Edwards' version of the biblical story from Genesis to Revelation but told through the eyes of the angels. It was mesmerizing, entertaining and totally thought provoking...truly one of those things that make you say, "Hmmm."

This came at a time when I was questioning my religious beliefs and was in need of an anchor....something to hold me firm. I thereafter understood why angels are referred to as "ministering spirits". They are directed to stand just outside of the physical realm and direct the lives of God's children. Throughout my life, I have had angels who came to comfort me in times of distress. I have had angels who empowered me with strength

Our guardian angels sometimes fly so high, they are beyond our sight...but they are always looking down upon us.

to defeat the enemy during spiritual battles. I have personally dispatched angels to my children in times of distress to protect and keep them safe.

One incident in particular occurred when my son, then 21 years old, was driving transport trucks long distances for a living. On one particular trip his truck developed engine problems on a deserted stretch of highway between Houston and Dallas. He called me around 3:00 a.m. and told me what was happening. He tried to reassure me that help was on the way and would be there in about two hours. Immediately the enemy began to bombard my mind with fear of all the terrible things that could occur. Feeling helpless, I drew upon the only source I knew and called upon God to dispatch angels to help and protect him. An hour or two later, he called to say that as he sat there alone, a man walked up to his truck and asked if he could help. My son responded that he was having engine trouble but a wrecker truck was on its way to assist him. The stranger then asked if he could sit there with him as he waited. This was a deserted area and my son was initially hesitant but felt unafraid of the stranger and agreed to allow him to sit with him. They sat and talked until the wrecker driver arrived and the stranger rode in the truck with my son to the next truck stop. My son got out of his rig to go and talk with the wrecker driver. When he turned to look at his truck and check on the stranger, no one was there. The stranger was not in the parking lot or inside the building. He was simply gone.

Many would try to offer a rational reason for the man's disappearance but belief is a matter of choice and I choose to believe that God answered my prayer and sent an angel.

Over the years, God has placed many other books in my path that gave insight into the character and purpose of angels. An angel is a spiritual being different from man in every way. I believe they were created by God long before the earth was created. They are heavenly spirits organized in a society whose purpose is to worship God and carry out His commands on Earth. They come to bring messages of hope and love from God to his children. They come to tell us that we have the power to grow and change...that we can heal and be healed. They want us to be whole, as God is whole, and filled with wisdom, knowledge, peace and love.

As you read this, perhaps you will ask, "How can I get an angel to come to my aid?" The answer is simple. Just Ask!

*We can live our lives
two ways.
One is living like
miracles never happen.
The other is living like
everything that
happens is a miracle.*

CHAPTER SEVEN

ALWAYS EXPECT A MIRACLE

When I talk about the Power of Prayer , I stress that prayer will bring about a change if that is what you desire. Sometimes that change comes as a result of natural occurrences over a period of time. There are other times, however, when change occurs supernaturally in a way that can only be termed *miraculous*. When this occurs, many believers view that miracle as an unexpected outcome and are in awe of God's power.

The word says that "Our God is an awesome God!" I believe this but where I differ with many believers is in my immediate expectation for Him to do something miraculous in every situation. God himself asked the prophet in Jeremiah 32:27 "Is anything too hard for me?" The answer is and always has been a resounding "No!" There is nothing that He is unable to do so I say to you "Always Expect a Miracle."

When God's glory spills over into the physical arena, we often experience a miracle. Sometimes it is prompted by a request made by a believer during a time of need. Other times it is divine intervention in a situation where God decides to just "show out" for a while. Both times, it is a demonstration of the supernatural.

Miracles are God's way of saying, "Stop worrying child, I got this."

Miracles have been plentiful in my life. I did not realize this in my youth because I thought all good people were blessed…a childish notion I know. I now realize that my acts of kindness, my giving, my sacrifice, my support of God's plan and my unshaken belief in the power of God sowed miracle seed that I was able to harvest in a time of need. When I understood this, I learned how to tap into the supernatural power of God. I received an open invitation in his Word to "prove him" or in other words "test him out". The outcome has been a continuous flow of miracles that have blessed my life and the lives of my family. Yes there have been challenges, but when a miracle is needed, a miracle is what God sends.

I have personal knowledge of the truth of this as I experienced a life-saving miracle in the fall of 2001. I was diagnosed with liver disease with the grim prognosis of limited life expectancy without a liver transplant. Few family members and even fewer of my friends knew this because I seldom mentioned it.. I refused to give life to the situation by speaking of it and chose instead to believe God for my healing. During worship services at my church one evening, Bishop Hilliard informed us that there would be a special healing service that next evening. I truly believed this to be my opportunity to get healed so I was in attendance expecting my miracle. My faith teaches that "believers can lay hands on the sick and they shall recover" so I waited patiently in line for my turn to be prayed for. This was not the first time I had sought God's help. Actually, it was about the hundredth time but my faith never wanned and I fully believed that night to be my miracle night. When the Man of God laid his hand upon me, I knew something miraculous had happened. My body, on the inside, felt different.

Over the next few days, my symptoms improved and a follow-up visit to my doctor showed my liver enzyme levels to be almost normal. When he inquired as to what I had been doing to show such improvement, I responded "praying for my healing." He merely smiled and said," Well, you keep praying because its working." That was twelve years ago and today, I continue to walk in divine health because of the miraculous power of God. Now, when someone tells me of an event that can only be termed "miraculous," I give God a "high-five" and say "You Go God!"

*Patience can be
defined as
intensity of purpose
with the ability to do,
yet having the power
to wait.*

CHAPTER EIGHT

YOU CAN'T RUSH THE SUNSHINE

Life requires that we spend some of our time wait-ing for things to happen. My Mom would say, "Girl, you can't rush the sunrise, it will all come in time." This would usually follow one of my many melt- downs when something did not go as I had so carefully planned. Nothing can be more exasperat-ing than coping with delays and disappointments whether we are adolescents or adults. As we move through life we must accept that everything will hap-pen when it is supposed to happen. Accepting that is what teaches us patience. We learn that worry, fear and anxiety are by-products of an impatient mind.

The key to patience trusts that inner presence, your spirit, to know exactly what must be done. It requires being able to hear and recognize that in-ner voice that gives direction and insight. It causes events to unfold divinely at just the right time.

The Word says, *"All things work together for our good." (Romans 8:28 KJV)* which should inspire us to patiently wait for things to work out, but so often does not. It's a natural tendency, when we encounter a situation that we cannot alter, to try to figure out a solution to the problem. I too am a solution thinker, but in doing so, I am often my own worst enemy. However, I have learned that instead of running off unprepared with a half thought out solution, the best course of action is often just to sit still and wait on God. In fact, the more hopeless a problem appears, the more difficult an obstacle seems, the more unwinnable a situation is, the greater God is glorified when it all finally works out in our favor. The hard part, in all of this, is learning to wait patiently.

We all know people who are easily irritated by even the smallest things. Invariably, they have a way of letting others know it, either by grumbling and complaining or they "Go Off" in total fury, shouting a stream of obscenities intended to let everyone within hearing distance know they have "Had It". The bulk of us can be found somewhere in between. We may not display our complete agitation on the outside, but inwardly we are churning with varying degrees of stress wishing that people would "get on with it, or get out of our way" so we can do our own thing. The problem is that "our thing" is often the wrong thing and only causes more problems.

It is so easy to become discouraged when things do not happen when we want them to happen. We live in a era where instant gratification is the norm, thanks to modern technology. Well, God does not operate a cosmic ATM machine passing out blessings when we punch in just the right code or pray just the right prayer. His thoughts are not our thoughts and our desires do not automatically become His emergency. Whether we believe it or not, even when it seems that nothing is happening, change is taking place, situations are being reversed and plans are being made. We may not feel it, or see it but our Faith will bring it to pass if we do not give up.

There is also a very sad truth to be learned from impatience. When we refuse to allow proper timing to unfold and stubbornly push hard enough, God will allow us to proceed on our own. The outcome is often disasterous because we tried to accomplish it within our own strength. The problem with this is that we will, thereafter, have to continue to manage the situation alone, without God's help.

Patience, for the most part comes with experience . It is built during those times of distress when we choose to sit silently and allow our Spirit to take command of a situation. Each display of patience gives us an increasing amount of strength to stand in any situation, when and wherever it arises. As we demonstrate our desire to wait patiently for an answer to our dilemma, we are also showing our trust in God to do what he said and "work everything out for our good." So, I suppose the moral is, *Be Still and Wait For Your Answer.* It will surely come and be right on time.

My faith will act like a bridge that takes me from where I am to where I want to go.

CHAPTER NINE

FAITH IS A SERVANT
BEST KEPT BUSY

When I heard Bishop I. V. Hilliard say "Faith is a servant that works best if it is kept busy", I admit that I laughed quietly to myself because it re-minded me of something my mother would always say.."Idle hands and an idle mind are the devil's workshop." As a child, I thought this meant that she had justified the reason I had to perform non-stop chores on the weekend. I, for one, felt that it was as close to child abuse as one could get without going to jail. She, on the other hand, believed that keeping a child's hands and mind busy would ultimately limit the amount of time he had to involve himself in less productive pursuits such as playing childish games and being mischievous. She, therefore, kept me busy at all times. I became her servant who worked tirelessly to carry out her wishes. After all, that is what a servant does!

It is the same concept if we view our faith as a servant. However, before you can begin to see faith as a servant you must first know what faith is. Webster defines faith as believing without proof. It is defined biblically as *"the substance of things hoped for; the evidence of things not seen." (Hebrews 11:1 KJV)*

Faith is not just belief without proof. It is also trust without reservation.

If faith has substance, then reasonably, it is possible for faith to be molded and remade to become that which you are hoping for. Is it not also reasonable to say that you can tell your faith to create a new car, a better job, a new home or more money? Once activated your faith gets busy to accomplish every goal you set before it. The busier it is kept, the more *hoped for things* it can create from things not seen. Now, that's a concept that makes you say, "Hmmm."

The true test of your faith is to "put it to work" for you. The Word says, *"If you have faith as small as a mustard seed, you can say to this mulberry tree, be uprooted and planted in the sea; and it will obey you." (Luke 17:6 KJV)* The point is, the God whose power regulates the universe would literally transport a mountain or a tree if there was a need to do so to illustrate the limitless power of Faith.

Each of you have dreams and desires that seem unattainable, or situations which appear to be beyond your natural ability to change. Faith is belief in something even when there is no physical evidence to support that belief. Faith is not based upon what you see but rather upon what God says he will do.

You may ask, "How is it possible to have this kind of faith?" If faith does not depend on tangible evidence, then how can a person ever be sure of its true existence? The answer is that it is not possible, humanly, that is. As humans we are limited in what we can conceive. Whatever our human mind produces is often sporadic and undependable. Human faith wavers and sometimes falters. The faith to "move mountains" is living faith and it is a gift of God. He has "given to each one a measure of faith (II Peter 1:1 KJV). That is what links us to Him.

Life is filled with obstacles that can seem as big as that mountain or a tree referred to in scripture. We all, from time to time, encounter situations and circumstances that are overwhelming. It is at that time that we must put our God given faith to work. You may not be able to see faith working on your behalf but you simply begin to act as if it is so and hold fast to your confession and belief in a positive outcome. Those actions keep your faith working to bring those dreams and desires to pass. Finally, when the goal is accomplished and you have "what you believed and said", that is not the time to give your faith a rest. Faith is a servant that works best under pressure. It can work without taking a break or needing a vacation. It will never tell you that something is impossible or cannot be done. It will stand with you during your most challenging struggles. It also does not even mind if you redirect it to help someone other than yourself. If you don't let it get lazy, but keep it busy, it will enable you to inherit all that you have been patiently waiting for.

Wisdom for Spiritual Strength

Talk to God in prayer and ask for strength each day. You will gain reassurance and confidence each time you stop and pray.

CHAPTER TEN

STOP, DROP AND PRAY

Prayer is the "supreme resource." When we have
nothing else at hand, we can always pray. It is
always appropriate, never out of season and never
out of style. Prayer is the pathway to peace because
it puts us into contact with God. It involves devel-
oping a friendship with God, much like David and
Abraham did.

Men and women from the beginning of time have
always felt an instinctive desire to look to a higher
power. We pray because we must. For many it is
not a normal activity because society has dulled
our appetite for it and we only pray when we find
ourselves in trouble. While God is not some kind of
"Cosmic Bellboy" he promises to answer our prayers
because his Word is on the line. He knows we are
helpless without Him. He only wishes we realized
it more often.

All of God's promises are conditional except one-
- to love us. There are, therefore, conditions required
for successful and effective praying. The first thing
we should understand is that prayer is more than

simply muttering a few words and then walking away expecting immediate results. The bible teaches that we can have confidence that those things we pray for will be granted when we pray according to God's will. We can then be assured that He hears us and will grant our desires. Before we can do this, however, we must first discover God's will. His will can be found in His word so we must find what the word says about our situation. Believe it or not, everything we have ever needed is addressed in His word. We simply need to search the scriptures on a consistent basis so that we know how to pray according to His word.

The passages below illustrate how to apply the word to various situations.

When You Are Afraid or Worried –
I thank you, Father, that you have given me the power to tread upon serpents and scorpions, and over all the power of the enemy and nothing shall by any means hurt me.
(Luke 10:19 KJV)

Father, Your word says that whatsoever I bind on earth shall be bound in heaven and whatsoever I loose on earth shall be loosed in heaven (Matthew 16:19 KJV)... so I bind fear and worry in the name of Jesus.

For Finances –
You are able to make all grace abound toward me so that I will always have all sufficiency in all things.
(II Corinthian 4:18 KJV)

You are doing exceedingly abundantly above all that I could ask or think according to the power that works within me.
(Ephesians 3:20 KJV)

What if you woke up this morning with only those things that you thanked God for on yesterday?

I choose to be careful for nothing because your Word says that by prayer and supplication all I have to do is make my requests unto you with thanksgiving (Philippians 4:6 KJV).

Because I am a giver, men give to me good measure, pressed down, shaken together and running over shall men give into my bosom.
(Luke 6:38 KJV)

For Faith–
Father, I choose to look not at the things which I can see but the things I cannot see: for the things which I see are temporary, but the things unseen are eternal.
(II Corinthians 4:18 KJV)

I believe that whatsoever things I desire when I pray, if I believe I will receive them, then I shall have them.
(Mark 11:24 KJV)

We receive the promise of the spirit thru faith.
(Galatians 3:13 KJV)

For Health and Healing –
Father, it is written in your Word that Jesus, who his own self bare our sins in his own body on the tree that we being dead to sins should live unto righteousness; by whose stripes we were healed.
(I Peter 2:24 KJV)

Praise the Lord, oh my soul and forget not His benefits who forgives all our sins and heals all our diseases.
   (Psalms 103:2-3 KJV)

For Wisdom –
Father, I thank you that you have destined and appointed me to come progressively to know your will. I thank you that the Holy Spirit abides permanently in me and guides me into all truth. I have the mind of Christ and hold the thoughts and feeling and purposes of His heart.
   (I Corinthians 2:12-16 KJV)

For Protection–
Father, you are my refuge and my fortress. No evil shall befall me, no accident shall overtake me, nor any plague or calamity comes near my home. You give your angels special charge over me to accompany, defend and preserve me in all my ways.
   (Psalms 91 KJV)

I thank you father that You are my confidence and will keep my foot from being snared by the enemy.
   (Proverbs 3:26 KJV)

As believers, we are told that when we pray according to God's will (His word) we know that He hears us and we can then expect to have those things that we ask of Him. This is because He has placed the truth, importance and impact of His word above everything…even His own desires. God's word is unchangeable. When we place a demand on that Word, it does not return to us void of power but accomplishes every thing that it is sent to accomplish.

Always use prayer as the main foundation of every endeavor. Seek God's direction through prayer before beginning anything and failure will not be an option. God desires that we are successful and He has not left us helpless. We have His word and His Spirit to guide us to insure our complete and total victory in life.

There is much we will never know, so breathe deeply and relax into the "not knowing". There is so much we do not have to know in order to live joyfully.

CHAPTER ELEVEN

GREET EACH DAY WITH A JOYFUL HEART

There will be days when you wake up feeling great, ready to stand and take on the world. Then there will be other days when you will wake up to bitterness in your Spirit that makes the whole world seem depressing. On those dark days, you need to remember that every day is a blessing to behold.

You must realize that the attitude with which you greet the day sets the pattern for what the day will be like. You choose to make your day pleasant or miserable. If you insist on starting your day feeling irritable, and with a bad attitude, more than likely the day will give you, in return, exactly what you began with. Sometimes bad things do happen to good people, but know that they often happen the way they should, at just the right time and to the right person. You can rest in the knowledge that you are equipped to handle it.

When we start the day displaying a spirit of joy, openness, peace and love, we put the universe on alert that we want more of the same. A day is too valuable to waste on misery and unhappiness.

When the day is spent, we can never regain the lost opportunity to share a smile, pray with someone, say

You have turned my mourning into joyful dancing. You have taken away my clothes of mourning and clothed me with Joy. Psalms 30:11

an encouraging word or help someone in need. There is a proverb that says, "100 years from now, it will not matter how rich or poor I was, the type of car I drove or the house I lived in, but the world will only be better if I made a difference in someone's life." That should be the ultimate purpose for each day.....to achieve as much as we can and touch as many lives as possible.

When we open ourselves to joy, we also open the door to light, laughter, strength and grace. All of these are gifts which come as a result of the joy we share. Sometimes joy is quiet and hidden. Other times joy will burst out in song and movement or in the act of creation...inviting us to dance and celebrate freely the goodness and beauty around us.

In order to live joyfully, we must learn to live one day at a time and stop fretting about the future. We must learn to make the most of the moment and understand that God has given us grace for today only. He has not given us tomorrow's grace. It will only be available when we get to tomorrow so there is no need to worry about future occurrences.

God gives us His joy but it is up to us to receive it and make use of it daily. It is one of the fruits of the spirit--Love, Peace, Joy, Long-suffering, Patience, Kindness, and Gentleness. When the scripture says, *"the joy of the Lord is your strength"(Nehemiah 8:10KJV)* it was letting us know that during troubling times we do not have the physical, emotional or spiritial strength to withstand the enemy's attack if we allow fear or sadness to overtake us. We then become vulnerable and easily defeatable. We are better equipped to deal with adversity when we approach the situation with the right attitude. We may not have all the answers but we can trust in the knowledge that our joy will be full at all times.

Joy is a cup overflowing that generously shares itself with all who are near. When we are joyful,we are exposed but unafraid. We are willing to unselfishly share the gift of love, hope and encourgement with others knowing that " *what we make happen for others, God will also make happen for us."* (Ephesians 6:7 KJV)

Obedience is making a decision to do as instructed even when it seems like an uneven exchange.

CHAPTER TWELVE

OBEDIENCE IS BETTER THAN SACRIFICE

There is a well-known proverb that says *"Train up a child in the way he should go, and when he is old he will not depart from it."*(Proverbs 22:6 KJV)   This may sound simple but, as a parent, I know that the "training " part is probably the most difficult thing to do in the child rearing process. Some children are receptive to training while others resist it with everything in them. I have found that the "free will" that God gave to each of us usually rises to the surface at the most inopportune times...especially where our children are concerned.

As creatures born with questions in our mouths, the natural inclination is to ask the question---WHY? Every three year old wants to know "why ?" and it does not end there. From that time forward, whenever an instruction is given to the child, the immediate response is to ask, "Why?"

Most parents do not desire and definitely do not need help in making parental decisions. That, however, does not stop our children from constantly seeking to direct their own paths.   Most do not buy in to the belief that our instructions should be followed *"just because I said so."*

We have all, without a doubt, heard the phrase, *"because I said so"* hundreds of times from our parents, teachers and others. The humbling part is that it is often spoken by someone with the intent to silence any and all resistance from the other person. Sometimes it works but most times it doesn't. It is at that time that the all too familiar, "why?" response usually rears its ugly head.

I have found that the only way to silence the "why?" is to make sure my children understand the tangible benefits derived from following my instructions. Maybe the benefit is a treat, a future reward, or delayed punishment. Nevertheless, that all too common question of "Why?" or "What's in it for me?" is fully addressed. Yet, isn't this the same way that we, as adults, also learn.

God has given us his written Word and often begins a passage with the phrase *"it is written"* or more commonly *"because I said so."* He desires that we accept what He has said without question and be willing to do as the Word instructs us. This is a simple enough request and should elicit no resistance.

Yet, this is also a perfect example of how the will of God does not automatically come to pass in the lives of His children. He wants us to believe and follow His instructions without question but many of us choose not to because we often can see no tangible (touchable, visible) benefit in doing so. God's response to our questions are answered with His "If....Then" directives.

- *"If we obey and serve Him, then we shall eat the good of the land." (Isaiah 1:19 KJV)*
- *"If a man's ways please God, (then) He will cause even his enemies to be at peace with him." (Proverbs 16:17 KJV)*
- *"If you obey me, (then) you shall be my treasured possession." (Exodus 19:5 KJV)*
- *"If my people will humble themselves and pray.. then will I hear from heaven ...and heal their land." (II Chronicles 7:14 KJV)*

One of my daily affirmations says "I believe God's word is true and will accomplish all that it says it will". In order for me to make this statement with any degree of confidence requires that I draw upon my past experiences in testing the truthfulness of His Word –a point of reference for future use.   As I remember the miracles that God has done in my life, I am convinced beyond measure that my obedience to his word is the primary channel which gives me access to the many blessings he has prepared for me.

Forgiveness is not something we do for others. We do it for ourselves so that we can heal and move on with our lives.

Chapter Thirteen

Let go of the Past

Forgiveness is a very remarkable concept. It means that while we may not forget an offense, we decide not to continue to punish the offender for his or her actions. It is sustained by mercy and requires that we love the person in spite of what he or she has done to us.

When we understand that offenses will come even in the best relationships, we must not be surprised when they actually happen. Invariably someone will say something that upsets us, or do something that displeases us. We will be made to feel ineffective, unqualified, disrespected or unloved at some point in our lives. However, the overall impact of such an offense can be greatly diminished if we have made provision beforehand for how we will deal with offenses. Without such a plan, when an offense occurs, unforgiveness settles in. Our heart then gets stuck at a point of pain that stays with us and rises each time we encounter the offender.

Unforgiveness is toxic and terrible. It gets worse as time passes because as the memory of that event infiltrates our hearts, bitterness, anger and frustration becomes the normal response.

Forgiveness brings freedom. Freedom from being controlled from the past. Freedom from emotional ties to the offender. Freedom to become whole and enjoy the fullness of life.

Be aware that it is not natural to harbor unforgiveness. It is a common practice but it is not man's natural state to be in a place of unforgiveness. It has the same debilitating effect as cancer. Left untreated, cancer spreads to other parts of the body destroying healthy cells and often causing irreparable damage, even death. It is the same with unforgiveness. Left untreated it spreads to other areas of our lives destroying healthy relationships and eventually causing irreparable damage... sometimes even the death of that and other relationships.

It must, therefore, be dealt with and eliminated in its early stages. If not, unforgiveness can become a shrine built around the alter of an experience that we worship and magnify forever. On the other hand, when we choose to deal with it, a minor offense never becomes a major offense. Our lives will then be better for having made provision for handling offenses before they occur.

You are asking, perhaps, how do you handle said offenses?

First, resist the temptation to ignore the offense. Sometimes we convince ourselves that we are being gracious when we chose to ignore an offense. Other times we don't act for fear of being hurt emotionally or even physically. We cannot allow such fear to subject us to inaction. Do not ignore what has offended you.

Next, address the offense in a systematic manner explaining the nature of the offense, why it offended you and what is required to resolve the matter. In other words address what happened and what you want the offender to do about it.

Finally, Let It Go! Choose not to constantly rehearse the offense. Forgive the offender and move on with your life. You cannot put energy into moving toward your destiny when you expend unnecessary energy going back to light up your history.

There are no magic forgiveness pills that will make the pain of an offense go away instantly. It is rather an ongoing process of choosing not to punish the offender and allowing them to regain your trust. Eventually, the pain lessens and the offense becomes a distant memory.

Wisdom for Personal Growth

Life is too short to waste it trying to live up to someone else's expectations. Listen to your inner voice and have the courage to follow your own heart.

CHAPTER FOURTEEN

YES YOUR LIFE HAS PURPOSE

Everyone has at one time or another asked themselves "why am I here? or "what is my purpose in life?" It is quite a question to ponder but believe it or not, we all have purpose. Some of us are quicker on the uptake and figure it out sooner than others. So many people do not discover their purpose until much later in life while others never seem to figure it out at all. Those are the sad ones who float aimlessly through life on the winds of chance, being tossed and thrown from one bad experience to another. Some would say that whatever they experienced was destined for them. I, unfortunately, do not agree. I believe that seeds of greatness are planted in each of us. Our choices, however, determine our eventual outcome. That being the case, we must agree with those writers who say, "It is true that God wrote our end from the beginning."

The Word says *"Before I formed thee in the belly, I knew thee...." (Jeremiah 1:5KJV)* The truth of that statement says that He knew who we were and what we were to become even before the moment of conception. Now, I am sure you will agree that concept takes the idea of "being connected" to new levels. God says that He predestined us to live a certain life. The concept of predestination is based upon God's foreknowledge of what is yet to come. This means He has written our beginning and end but whatever happens in the middle is left up to us. This is why knowing your purpose is so important.

Fulfilling your potential begins with uncovering the gifts and skills with which you were blessed. Your natural talents and abilities always contribute and correspond to your purpose and destiny. Some talents are more easily identifiable than others. Those who sing, compose, and play instruments often see their roles as singers and musicians. On the other hand, those with no easily recognizable talent question their purpose. The questions to consider in those instances are (1) What is burning inside of your heart? (2) What are you obsessed with when you dream dreams for God? and (3) What has God spoken personally to your heart?

Take time to reflect in silence. The purpose and destiny that God has called you to is the primary voice on the inside of you. Take time to get to know yourself and you will find that God's will is as close as your most persistent thoughts and deepest desires.

When you are living your life according to your purpose, you position yourself so that you can be more effective in life. You are then able to walk into your destiny recognizing and eliminating those unforseen and unnecessary roadblocks along the way. When you know your purpose, you will find that sometimes you must alter certain circumstances because they are not escalating you toward your destiny. There will be relationships you must redefine and alter, jobs you will have to leave, habits you must break, and things you will have to give up. When that happens, you must stop looking in the rear-view mirror of your life at where you have been and start looking forward to your destiny before you.

God's design was for you to play a particular role and fit into a particular plan. Your personality, your character, your passion and insights were crafted for a master plan. You must therefore take time to study and evaluate who you are, why you are here and where you are going. Do not expend unnecessary energy dwelling on those things that do not guide you to your destiny. Live your life consciously and courageously with purpose so that others will see a reflection of God's love in you.

How to get it Done

- Decide what it is that you want.
- Trust your spirit.
- Plan prayerfully, prepare purposefully, proceed positively, pursue persistently.
- Be flexible, adjust for mistakes in judgment.
- Do the best you can, where you are, with what you have
- When it doubt, pray. Know that help is on the way.

CHAPTER FIFTEEN

LIFE'S JOURNEYS BEGINS WITH HALF PACKED BAGS

One of the greatest challenges I deal with each time I try to get packed for a vacation is what to take for the journey. I am by nature a frugal person so I try to travel with the least amount of items so that the weight does not slow me down or tire me out. I try to pack those items necessary for the journey but I always leave something important out. Trying to plan for every possible eventuality is really hard to do but we try nonetheless. Invariably, however, there is always something we need that is not packed in our bags....and so it is with life.

As children, if we are lucky, we are groomed, molded, trained and auditioned on how to prepare for each journey we will take in our life. Some say fill your bags with education, courage, strength, perseverance and things of that nature and you can make things happen that will benefit you. Others say, simply place goodness and love in those bags and you will be blessed with everything else along the way. The stout of heart say, arm yourself with boldness and fearlessness and you can take what you want regardless of the consequences. We really do not know which to pack so we decide to pack a little bit of everything. Surely then we are fully prepared for life's journey.

The path, however, takes us through situations where we often have no remedies in our bags. One day we encounter a situation and all of our courage, perseverance, goodness, love and fearlessness is of little use. There is nothing in our humanly packed bags that seems to solve the problem. Like a child, we find ourselves alone and unprepared.

Life is a journey filled with many lessons, hardships, and joys that will lead us to our ultimate destiny. The road will not always be smooth. In fact, all throughout our travels, we will encounter many challenges. Some of these challenges will put our courage,strength and faith to the test. How we handle the challenging times will often depend on which source we consult for help. The Word says that *"No eye has seen or ear has heard, or mind conceived what God has prepared for those who love Him but has revealed it to us by His Spirit."* *(ICorinthians 2:9 KJV)*

We may not have all that we require when we first approach life's paths but revelation is given at the appointed time and we can expect the direction and assistance needed. The glorious thing is that we are always given more when we are "on our way" than when we initially begin our journey.

If you are one of those who "got connected to the source" early in your life, then prayer will bring physical and spiritual provisions as you require them. It will not matter if you have half packed bags. Your faith will be the channel whereby all your needs will be met and you will always have something greater for the journey. You will have a covenant promise that you will be *"blessed in the land as you (journey to) possess it."(Deuteronomy 1:8 KJV)* You will not need to rely on your own resources or "what's in the bag" but know that there will always be someone along the way who is positioned to help you. You can stand on the promise that *"what things so ever you desire when you pray believe you receive them and you shall have them."* *(Mark 11:24 KJV)*

At the bottom of the hill, the little engine said, "I think I can, I think I can. At the top of the hill, the little engine said..."I can and I did"!

CHAPTER SIXTEEN

YOU ARE ONLY ONE THOUGHT AWAY FROM SUCCESS

Eli Whitney thought there was a more efficient way to process cotton so he invented the cotton gin in 1794. Edwin Budding thought there was an easier way to cut his grass so he invented the lawnmower in 1830. Mary Anderson thought there needed to be a way to clear water from a car's windshield, so she invented the windshield wiper in 1905. Betty Graham thought there was a neater way to correct typing errors so she invented Liquid Paper in 1979. The list of inventors, past and present goes on. Some of them we are familiar with while others are more obscure, but their inventions are no less important. Everything we currently enjoy was first a thought before it became reality. Somebody thought to make it all.

When God created Man, he made us in His image and gave us His character and taught us to be creative. He taught us that we could think our world into existence. He did not, however, give us the finished products we would need in our world. Instead, He gave us natural resources such as trees, air, water, soil and sunlight along with creative ideas to create chairs, cars, clothes, food and shelter. Out of our head comes our creativity, our strength, our wisdom which ultimately determines our success.

In order to be successful, we must have courage to think thoughts beyond our own ability. I have heard it said that we are often given more insight while we are on our journey than when we first begin. Thoughts are the seed of the mind and will produce after its own kind, blossoming into action while it is creating the fruit of opportunity or circumstance. Good productive thoughts will bear good productive actions creating good opportunities. On the other hand, negative thoughts will produce negative actions creating negative circumstances. Usually, people will not attract what they want but rather what they think. That is why the Word says, *"As a man thinketh in his heart, so is he."* *(Proverbs 23:7KJV)*

There is a battle going on daily which most people are not even aware of. It is not the battle for land and birthrights in the Middle East or for freedom in Africa. Instead it is a battle for something more valuable...our minds. The enemy knows that if he can control how we think, he can control our lives.

We must therefore renew our mind daily with those divinely inspired thoughts which affirm who we are and what we are capable of accomplishing. Many refer to these as Positive Affirmations or Confessions designed to build our self image and change our perceptions. Listed below are those which I quote to encourage and inspire myself. Perhaps, you too will find them helpful. Why not give it a try!

Personal Affirmations:

- I accept, acknowledge and embrace everything about me.
- I do not fret or have anxiety about anything.
- I reap a good harvest from the soil of my mind.
- I am divinely guided at all times and I know exactly what to do.
- I am limited not by what I see but by what I believe.
- God's strength, wisdom, power and love covers me and is expressed thru me.
- The harvest I reap will be measured by the seeds I sow.
- Today I will practice the art of listening to my Spirit.
- My thoughts are agreeable to His will so my plans are established and succeed.
- My Faith will make perfect that which concerns me.

Ralph Waldo Emerson said "When we make a decision, the universe conspires to make it happen." We can conclude, therefore, that we create our world with the words of our mouth.

We must realize that we "have not because we ask not". So we must begin daily to ask God for creative ideas and inspiration for witty inventions. Finally, we must believe that we shall receive all that God has for us and live in daily expectation of those blessings.

Life is...

Opportunity...Benefit from it
A Journey...Walk it
A Promise...Fulfill it
Beautiful...Appreciate it
A Joke...Laugh at it
A Song...Sing it
A Challenge...Meet it
Wonderful...Enjoy it
Precious...Don't Waste it

CHAPTER SEVENTEEN

IT'S OK TO FALL SOMETIMES

The other day, I sat and watched my, then, nine month old grandson stand and walk across the room. Just a few days before, he had been crawling around on all fours and seemed perfectly contented to do just that. But that particular day had been his first day at the day care center and he was the only baby in his class that was not walking. As it was his first day, the center director was gracious enough to allow me to sit with him until he felt confident enough to stay on his own.

I watched as he crawled over to various toys and pulled himself up to stand beside the other children. I beamed with pride as he held on with all of his strength to not topple over as he stood among them. When he would get tired, he would return to his knees and crawl back to me. Little did I know as he watched the other babies closely that he was building his determination to walk as well. After he returned home at the end of the second day, he sat watching his brothers play with a red ball. This, no doubt, intrigued him and suddenly he stood and took several steps across the room. He stumbled and fell but got back up to try again. He bumped his head, pulled things over and grabbed hold of anything and anyone within reach to stay on his feet. By the end of the day, with quite a few extra bumps, bruises and scratches he was walking the full length

> *Courage does not always roar. Sometimes courage is the quiet voice at the end of the day that says, "I'll try again tomorrow."*

of the room without falling. By the end of the week, he was walking around his classroom with the other babies proud as could be. Yes, he would still fall, but it did not stop him from getting up to try again and again.

I wonder, at what point did we, in growing up, manage to lose that fierce desire to succeed. Most of us consider ourselves more capable than a toothless toddler but I think the toddler knows something that we do not....it is OK to fall sometimes. It does not matter how many times you fall...you simply have to get back up. The funny thing about falling is that the more you fall, the less time it takes to get back on your feet the next time.

I sat and pondered the simple process of falling and afterwards arrived at the following hypothesis. For the novice trying to walk, the first fall is the most tramatic. It seems to knock more wind from us and hurts a bit more as it is often a surprise and a bit of an embarrassment. The second fall, however, hurts a bit less, leaves us frustrated, but only requires a bit of concentrated effort to stand again. By the third, fourth and fifth fall you are able to sense that you are about to fall and quickly look for something or someone to soften your fall. Around the tenth fall, when you see you are about to stumble, you stop before your next step, regain your balance then move ahead carefully. You have by then come to realize that falling is just a normal consequence in the process of learning to walk. Hence, we have heard countless times "You must crawl before you walk" spoken usually as a form of admonition given to one who is impatient with a particular process. If you consider the plight of the toddler and what he learned as he endeavored to succeed, perhaps you too will agree that sometimes falling is a necessary step in the learning process. You simply have to keep getting up.

Wisdom for Relationships

Who we really are is often well hidden from who we pretend to be. Of all the treasure, often the last to be dug up is one's real self.

CHAPTER EIGHTEEN

CHANGE BEGINS WITH ME

The distressing truth about relationships is that most of us go into them thinking that we can change the person we are with. We see in the other person what we perceive as flaws and take it upon ourselves to make them better. In our heads, given enough time, we believe we can fix what is wrong with them.

If we believe that our steps in life are ordered and our destiny is there for us to walk in, then we must accept that the people we attract into our life are a reflection of who we are. They are a product of our intelligent choice. They often display a side of us we are unable to see or are unwilling to acknowledge. The very thing we do not like about our mate is most likely the thing we need to change in ourselves. On the other hand, the thing we love about our mate is often that hidden, undeveloped or unrecognized thing we have yet to find in ourselves. The scientists had it right when they said "opposites attract." They did not, however, state that opposites were not meant to be together. The "being together" is what requires commitment and a decision to support our flawed mates rather than trying to fix them.

There is a major difference in fixing and supporting our mates. Fixing is telling them all the things that are wrong with them and how they should change or adjust them. Supporting is recognizing that you are two different people with different viewpoints and accepting those differences. Fixing is requiring them to do things your way. Supporting is allowing your mate to make their own choices. Fixing is pointing out every failure they have ever encounterd in life. Supporting is reassuring them and being available to help them the next time. Fixing is nagging. Supporting is nurturing. Fixing is showing anger when things get tough. Supporting is knowing things will get better.

Striving for perfection in a relationship is like trying to live an error-free life…it is nearly impossible. Mind you, I said "nearly" impossible because we all know that with God, all things are possible. Yet, for the most part we will all make mistakes and we will all experience strain and stress in our dealings with other people. We simply must realize that perfection runs two ways. It is pointless to spend an inordinate amount of time being frustrated by other people's thoughts or behaviors. Ultimately, we can only make our desires known and leave it to the other person to make personal adjustments as needed. We must support another independent thinking individual's right to "be or not to be" the person we desire them to be.

No one can give us what we do not already have. If we are not at peace with ourselves, we will not find peace in someone else. If we lack compassion and understanding. we will not receive the compassion and understanding we desire from others. The thing about relationships is that they run both ways. You must first be willing to "pay forward" that which you want in return. No one can make us happy if we choose to be unhappy. Before we can require perfection in others, we must first be perfect in ourselves. When I strive for a better me, then I will be too busy to notice that there are faults to be overcome in a better you.

*Don't expect
everyone to
understand your
journey
especially if they have
never had to walk your
path.*

CHAPTER NINETEEN

ENJOY THE RIDE OR GET OFF MY TRAIN

It is sometimes hard to get others to follow our train of thought. It does not matter how hard we try, they simply refuse to understand and accept our point of view. Reason and rational falls upon deaf ears and our numerous explanations are derailed even before the train gets started. To continue on that track is useless so stop trying. It is your train and you are both engineer and conductor.

Without intending to, we often allow other people's opinions to dominate our lives at times. The question becomes, why do they matter so much to so many of us? Even the most independent-minded among us can have a hard time not caring what others think; especially those certain others whom we are close to.

Being overly affected by other people's opinions is always an indication that we have lost connection to our own inner wisdom. Instead of trusting the voice of our spirit we look for further confirmation from others that what we are doing is right. Always looking to others for guidance will only feed those feelings of insecurity. It is practically impossible to get even one other person to agree with *most* of what we do. We all know people who go from friend to friend, asking for that person's opinion, but are never quite able to accept any answer as the truth. The reason is that the only truth is the one that is offered by our own inner spirit.

Believe in yourself and all that you are. Know that there is something inside you that is greater than any obstacle.

Resident within each of us is an inner spirit that directs our conscious mind. Through that connection, we can gain insight and knowledge of what to do in every situation. When we allow ourselves to be guided by our inner voice, we often find that other's opinions are only of very minor consideration. In fact when you are guided by the unwavering wisdom of your inner knowing, your truth is securely established in every area and the opinions of others have very little impact.

Noted speaker and author Les Brown once said "Other people's opinions do not have to become your reality." This is particularly significant as it was shared by a person who was labeled a slow-learner and placed in special education classes. Les, however, refused to believe what others said about his abilities. He had big dreams. He had no formal education beyond high school, yet he had determination and persistence. His passion for learning enabled him to further his education by self-education. Today, in spite of the opinions of others he is a respected and sought after motivational speaker affecting the lives of others.

Always know that you determine the path your train of thought will follow. If others disagree, then so be it. The path to success will have enough warning signs, pitfalls, detours and objections. You do not need to invite more aboard your train. No one can judge your path unless they have walked your journey so tell them to either sit down and enjoy the ride or" GET OFF MY TRAIN!" As engineer, the direction your train will take is totally up to you. It will, no doubt, be an adventuresome journey but that will only add to the excitement of seeing the many sights and awesome scenery along the way to your destiny.

Each of us brings to the world something unique...who we are, what we choose to do, our own unique talents gifts.
Know that someone, somewhere will benefit from knowing you.

CHAPTER TWENTY

LOVE THEM BUT DON'T LOSE YOURSELF

How many times have you met a couple who mirrors one another's actions? They speak with the same intonation and voice inflections. They can complete the other's sentences or give the other's opinion on every topic. They even coordinate their clothing colors and styles. Someone might simply conclude that they "Just know each other well." Not So! The real truth is that one of them has lost themselves in that relationship.

When we enter into relationships we think our ideal mate is someone who is exactly like us. We want that person to be an extension of our beliefs, values and ideals which is reasonable at the outset. However, people sometimes grow in different directions and different is not necessarily bad. We can be different from one another in many good ways. We must choose to accept those differences and love one another in spite of them.

It can sometimes be hard to maintain what defined you as a person before the relationship began. Perhaps you enjoyed solitary walks in the park or digging through old antique shops for knickknacks and old books. If so, then that is what you should still be doing now. "I" may now have become "We", and two may have become one but you have to exert conscious effort not to lose yourself in the equation.

Being involved in a relationship can be both exciting and exhilirating. The initial feelings of infatuation can be addictive, literally. You find yourself wanting to spend every moment possible with that person. As a couple you blend together to the point where one or both of you have to adapt your lifestyle to include the other person. Ordinarily, this is acceptable but not to the point where it becomes necessary to sacrifice your self-identity. Compromise and sacrifice are necessary in any relationship but too much sacrifice can lead to feelings of resentment and the ultimate demise of the relationship. There are ways to maintain a long-term relationship without giving up the essence of who you are.

One of the most important things to remember is that you don't have to do everything together. If you always occupy each other's space, there is no freedom of thought, no element of surprise and no mystery in the relationship. You have nothing new to say because you have no unique experiences to share.

Secondly, nurture and stay connected to the friends and important people in your life. They will enhance your life in ways that your partner does not.

Finally, build in some quiet time for yourself. Go see that new play in town or sit alone and read a book. Take frequent breaks away from each other regularly. Give your mate an opportunity to appreciate your uniqueness.

Relationships are wonderful and truly have their benefit but completely erasing yourself to accommodate the needs of another person is totally unacceptable. What makes relationships so amazing is that you enter into them with your whole self, your personality, experiences and individuality. Why give up any part of that just to satisfy another's quirks? Holding on to a bit of who you are can be amazingly beneficial to the relationship as it will remind them of why they chose to be with you in the first place. Ultimately, it will give each person a sense of self that time cannot erase or displace.

When we summon the courage to take ownership of our experiences, to see them just as they are, to feel the emotions they bring, we will recover the blue-prints of our lives. We will face our fears and exorcise the demons that created them. We will become honest with ourselves and lay the foundation upon which strength is built.

CHAPTER TWENTY-ONE

THE BUCK STOPS WITH ME

The phrase "The buck stops with me ," was made famous by President Harry S. Truman in the 1930's. It was made during a time of political turmoil and referred to the fact that the President has to make decisions and take responsibility for those decisions. It was used recently by President Barack Obama as he took ownership of the problems facing America following his election in 2008. In both instances, the statement signaled the end to "placing the blame" on someone else for actions we take and decisions we make. Likewise, we must apply that same axiom to our personal relationships.

Each of us enter into relationships expecting all circumstances to rival perfection if not be actually perfect. Whether it is an intimate relationship with a mate, a business relationship with an associate or a familiar relationship with a friend or relative, we still want everything to proceed without any complications. Human nature, however, has a way of bringing with it emotions and feelings that are not always consistent with our plans for the relationship. Anger, hurt, resentment, disappointment can often surface at the most inopportune time and change the tenor of our relationships with others.

One of the hardest things that we, as humans, must learn is that we cannot control how others will react in various situations. The only thing we have control over is our own inner thoughts and outer emotions. Whether we choose to respond "in kind" with the same degree of emotion or whether we choose to take responsibility for assuring a positive outcome is a choice that must be made. That choice will then be either the catalyst for resolution or the beginning of a crisis within the relationship.

During difficult times in a relationship, we must be willing to address the problem "head on". It can never become one of those debilitating scenarios where "if we don't discuss it, it does not exist". Each person in the relationship must take accountability for his or her actions. We can provide information, ideas and solutions to our loved ones and associates, but the desire to change must come from the individual. When we hold ourselves accountable, we claim our personal power to change things for the better and create much different results.

If our relationships are not going as expected, we need to examine our own behavior. Often people will "mirror" our attitude at a subconscious level. If we are angry or resentful, it will be evident in how we speak and the body language displayed. We can then expect the other person to respond in an angry and resentful manner. The reality is that we can determine the outcome by how we approach the problem. We must make a quality decision to forgive, cease from placing blame on others, and respect the other person's inherent individuality. To maintain balance in every relationship, understand that other's actions do not define the whole picture. It is rather our own response to those actions that becomes the tapestry upon which outcomes are weaved. The choice is yours. In order to be the catalyst for change, always remember that "the buck stops here."

The thing always happens that you really believe in; the belief in the thing is what makes it happen.

CHAPTER TWENTY-TWO

GET OVER YOUR B.S.

Your Belief System (B.S.), those truths about yourself and others, is a product of your personal perceptions and experiences. It determines the way you approach life. If you really want to know what you believe, look at the people, conditions and the situations in your immediate environment. They are a reflection of your B.S.--the result of your own intelligent choice.

We are all works in progress. What we believe will be either positively or negatively affected by those same people, conditions and situations in our immediate environment. That is why it is so very important to carefully monitor who and what we allow to speak into our lives. We have all heard stories of how people with just a dream and their belief in their ability to achieve it became successful entrepreneurs. They are no different from you or anyone else. They simply had a belief system that supported their expectations for great success.

Many of the limitations you will face in life are self-imposed based upon what you believe. What you believe about yourself can keep you locked tightly behind your fears or thrust you forward into living your dreams.   Ernest Holmes said "Change your thinking, change your life." Mark Twain however said it better. "If you think you can, you can. If you think you can't, you're right."

Limiting beliefs act as filters of the reality God says is possible for you. You can normally recognize them because they usually begin with the word "but". How often have you heard someone say, "I want to start my own business, but…." or "I'd like to finish my degree, but…" or "I need a new car, but… The reality of each statement said that each was possible, yet a limiting belief immediately offered a reason why success was not possible. What you believe and the way you see the world will ultimately determine what you achieve in life.

Most of us form beliefs because they simplify our lives. When you were told as a child that the stove was hot, you incorporated that information into your belief system and now as an adult you are careful around the stove so as not to get burned. This is an example of a positive belief that simplifies your life and protects you from harm. Every opinion you have and the way you see the world is influenced by your beliefs. Many of them have a positive affect but just as many, if not more, have a negative affect. If, during the course of your day, you experience negative emotions about a seemingly insignificant occurence, it is a result of your belief system. If you find yourself unable to relate to a particular individual or group, it is because of your belief system.

Identifying and eliminating limiting beliefs is not

always an easy thing to do. Usually, you believe in something because you have evidence to support that belief. Perhaps it was instilled by your parents or some other significant person. Maybe it was the result of something you read or heard. In any case, the fact remains that you have the absolute ability to choose what you want to believe, how you want to live and what you want to do. As you strive to eliminate negative or limiting beliefs, make a conscious effort to reflect on your or another's experiences that support an empowering belief.

As your belief system changes and empowering beliefs become the norm, your life will change quite perceptibly as you begin to expect positive outcomes. Whatever you expect to happen will become your own self-fulfilling prophecy because you will always act to achieve what you expect. At the same time, cultivate those relationships that enhance your belief system. Never allow another's beliefs to alter your perceptions. Believe in what is possible for you. If what you believe is holding you back, it is now time to get over your B.S (Belief System) and make a change for the better.

*It is more important
what you think of
yourself than what
others think of you.
Your self-esteem is
built upon the words
of your mouth alone.*

CHAPTER TWENTY-THREE

WHAT SAYEST THOU OF THYSELF?

It constantly amazes me the answers I get when I ask the question, "How are you today?" Many people will answer it simply by saying "Fine", or "O.K, I guess". Others will give you their latest medical, financial, and psychological updates with an offer to "show you their scar".

Because we speak our world into existence with the words of our mouth, it is vitally important that we monitor closely what we say in response to the above question. So the next time someone asks you how you are, why not try this answer on for size.

"I am perfect. I am dynamite. I am whole. I am complete. I am lovable and busy loving others. I have it all together and am doing well. I am basking in the riches of life. I am prosperous in all that I do. I am wise. I am strong. I am a miracle worker expecting a miracle right now. I am at peace with my life and the world is at peace with me. I am wealthy; I am abundantly supplied at all times. I am living by pure grace. I am a believer always standing in faith. Now, how are you doing, ?"

A Mother's Prayer

My child...
May the Lord bless and
protect you.
May the Lord smile on you and
be gracious to you.
May the Lord show you His
favor and give you His peace.

Numbers 6:24-26 NLT

Wisdom for Increase

You are anointed to acquire when you sow seed for supernatural abundance and live in daily expectation of increase.

CHAPTER TWENTY-FOUR

SEED TIME AND HARVEST

In my house, I taught my children from infancy to adulthood that in order to gain something, they had to first give something. As toddlers, they were taught respect and the benefit of obedience. They were taught tolerance and unselfishness. As adolescents, they were taught to take ownership of their actions and the benefit of working for rewards. They were taught how to be good stewards over those rewards they were given and how to share their increase with others. As teenagers and young adults, all of the previous lessons learned were then put to the test and they were taught how to place a demand on the seeds that had previously been sown into their lives.

You see, I recognized from the beginning that their hearts and lives were merely gardens. Whatever I planted, I could expect that thing to be multiplied and returned to me in kind. If I planted love, patience, tolerance, joy, unselfishness, and respect, I could expect a harvest of the same. On the other hand, if I had planted hatred, disrespect, sadness,

107

selfishness and anger, my children would have planted and cultivated those negative traits into their heart and lives.

The principle of seed time and harvest has been around since the beginning of time. The Word says *"As long as the earth endures, seed time and harvest, cold and heat, summer and winter, day and night shall never cease."(Genesis 8:22 KJV)* It is a divine ordinance that we are governed inexplicably by the law of seed time and harvest or as we know it, "sowing and reaping." The unfortunate thing is that most of us are conditioned from birth to always expect and desire to reap. We want what we want when we want it, without delay. We completely overlook the undeniable truth that sowing is the only thing that makes it possible.

As you survey your life, whatever you lack, you must be willing to sow or "do" something to attain it. Ask yourself how you want to be treated , then that is how you are to treat others. Ask yourself where you want to go in your career, then begin to cultivate relationships with successful others. Ask yourself what level of financial prosperity you desire and begin contribute and sow into to the vision of other individuals. All of these are representative of the type of seed that is required to bring about a plentiful harvest in every area of your life. Without seed, it is impossible to bear fruit.

Throughout the bible, we see countless instances where God required a sacrificial gift before granting a prayed for blessing. The simple truth is that we are not blessed just to be able to live a lavish life. We are instead blessed to be a blessing to others. The end result can also be found in scripture. *"Give and it shall be given to you, pressed down shaken together and running over shall men give into your bosom."(Luke 6:38 KJV)* It is only after such a process that we can begin to place a demand on the seed we have sown. Increase in the area of career success, finances, health, and relationships are harvests for which we must have previously sown some type of seed. Only then can we expect a supply that will be able to fill to the full that which we require.

The greatest discovery of all time is when a man realizes that he can change his life by simply changing the way he thinks.

CHAPTER TWENTY-FIVE

NO BARRIERS, NO LIMITS

Each of us have at one time or another heard the saying " the only limitations are those that are in my own mind." If this is a true statement, then why is it that so many people fail to reach their full potential? Why do so many people experience a feeling of being stuck in a situation, without hope of ever getting up or out? Why do so many feel out of control and unable to change some of the negative situations in their lives? Why is it not possible for them the simply think their way into success?

The answer to this question is relatively simple. The people we described above are those individuals who, for whatever reason, do not choose to accept responsibility for their lives. Instead, they choose to blame someone else for the cause of their station or circumstance in life. Each of us have either met or personally known someone who feels as though they have no choices. They are stuck in a bad job, relationship, business, neighborhood, climate or way of life that they cannot seem to alter. This seems quite incongruent with nature as we are not trees stuck in the ground somewhere. We can move and change whenever we choose to. That being the case, why then don't we choose to? Perhaps fear, comfort, procrastination, other's emotional manipulation or simply our acceptance of our situation keeps us bound.

The truth is that each of us come into this world headed for greatness in some way. Initially, we were all engineered for success at birth but conditioned for failure along the way. We have forgotten whose image we were created in and that we were given His spirit and His mind with the power to create anything we desire. Each of us must realize that we can do whatever we put our minds to just as long as it is followed by corresponding action. Certainly we can expect to encounter barriers from time to time but we should not allow ourselves to become discouraged. The other day, I heard Bishop Hilliard say, "barriers which resist movement are only designed to deceive, delay and cause doubt. Your strength will be in the knowledge that you have been empowered to remove all barriers and self-imposed limits with the words of your mouth and a belief in your ability to accomplish whatever you desire."

Just as it is important that we see ourselves as God sees us, it is equally important that we say what God's words says about us. In previous chapters we stressed that "we have what we say" so we should use our words carefully. We create our world with the words of our mouth so we can choose whether to bring to life the good things God has in store for us. Because our words have seed potential we must take steps to plant them cafefully. No farmer haphazardly sows cotton seed where he wants potatoes to grow. Like the farmer, we must first decide what we want our harvest to be and begin to sow the right seed. Even before the first sprout, we must believe that we are blessed, act like we are blessed and continue to speak those blessings into existence. God has already equipped us with everything we need to live a prosperous life. He has planted seeds filled with potential, possibilities, and prosperity and all we need to do is identify and eliminate those self-imposed barriers to our success. God says that we are more than conquerors so that means we already have all the wealth, wisdom, and power of a warrior who has won the battle. We only need to begin to live that prosperous and victorious life He has set before us.

I will establish my covenant between me and you and your descendents......I will strenghten you and help you...I will up-hold you with my righteous hand.

(Genisis 17:7, Isaiah 41:10 KJV)

CHAPTER TWENTY-SIXTH

UNDERSTAND YOUR COVENANT CONNECTION

The time was rapidly passing and the date of his departure was quickly approaching but the young man was still feeling anxious about his decision to accept the new position as District Manager offered by his employer. This job offer was the answer to a prayer and confirmation of the company's faith in him. The only problem was that to accept the position, he would be required to move to another state. This would entail uprooting his entire family and leaving the home he had made in his current community, not to mention , leaving other family members and close friends.

For as long as he could remember, he had never lived more than one or two hours away from home which provided a sense of security for him. It was not so much that he needed to be near home for himself. Instead, there was comfort in knowing he was near enough to care for his parents and significant others. His deep sense of responsibility to family directly affected any decision he might make. The one thing he had learned as he grew into manhood was that he was not his own source of supply. He understood that there was a greater one that directed every area of his life and upon whom he could depend in times of despair. This was certainly a time of despair so he decided to go straight to the source—his Bible. The young man knew that his faith in this situation could not become rock-solid until he fully understood the details of that relationship.

As he studied his bible, he learned that there were benefits to which he was entitled because of his relationship with God. Those benefits were his because of the covenant commitment God had made with man as far back as the time of Adam. That covenant was a formal, solemn and binding agreement between God and mankind and it guaranteed God's involvement in all things concerning man. God had made a promise, a pledge and was now obligated to respond.

The young man knew that he would need to delve deeper if he was to find an answer to his question. His search led him to many chapters and numerous verses which told of God's promises to those who believed. He learned that as a child of God, he could rest on His promises to bless, heal, deliver, save and prosper him and his family. He was able to find scripture upon scripture to support the fact that God was committed to keeping his covenant promises. As he meditated on what he had learned he was overjoyed by the realization that those promises were more spectacular than anything he ever could have imagined as evidenced by those words which said:

"I will establish my covenant between me and you and your descendants after you throughout this generation for an everlasting covenant to be God to you."

"(Genesis 17:7 KJV)"

It was simply mind boggling for him to realize that the God who created heaven and earth, who parted the waters and placed the sun and the stars in the sky was committed to caring for him. The prophet Jeremiah explained what this meant. He quotes:

"They will be my people and I will be their God….I will not turn away from doing good to them..I will rejoice in doing good to them….with all my heart and with all my soul." *(Jeremiah 32:38-41 KJV)*

The young man concluded that if God was truly his God, then all of his omnipotence and all of his omniscience was actively engaged all the time to do good for him in all the circumstances of his life. With that revelation, God swallowed up the tension, fear and doubt that had been plaguing him and brought forth a great calm that made his decision to follow his dreams easy to accept. As he closed his bible he was reminded of God's Word which said:

"Do not fear, for I am with you. Do not be dismayed for I am your God. I will strengthen you and help you. I will uphold you with my righteous hand."

(Isaiah 41:10. KJV)

The amazing thing is these spectacular promises cannot be earned but they can be believed and if you believe them, everything changes.

About the Author

As far back as she remembers, LaVerne H. Harris often found herself somewhere in her home with a book in her hands. Always an avid reader, it was no surprise that the natural progression for her would be into the world of writing. From childhood she knew instinctively that books would occupy a great part of her life so it is no surprise to see her now authoring her own novels.

A native Texan, she grew up in the 50's as the younger of two children in the small coastal town of Bay City. She went on to pursue a degree from Texas Woman's University in the field of Education. Not being one to follow traditional paths, after graduation she went to work for the U. S Department of Labor as an Administrator with a migrant farm worker education program. After 25 years of impacting the lives of many students she became a high school teacher until her recent retirement.

Now she lives quietly with her husband of 40 years with a legacy of two children and ten grand children. When LaVerne isn't working on her next story you can find her puttering around in her flower garden, curled up with a book somewhere, or simply spending quality time with her family.

Her first book, Priceless Pearls, brings to the forefront her spiritual upbringing and the faith that has sustained her throughout her life. For her, it is the culmination of years of standing and believing in a power greater than herself. LaVerne invites you, the reader, to sit back and enjoy this literary journey with her.

www.ingramcontent.com/pod-product-compliance
Lightning Source LLC
LaVergne TN
LVHW051247080426
835513LV00016B/1779

* 9 7 8 0 6 1 5 7 7 4 1 2 1 *